# Coils of the Yamuna

Acknowledgments:
The Author would like to thank the Manitoba Arts Council for the Travel Grant which allowed him to travel in India.


Design by John Weier and Joe Blades
Printed and bound in Canada by Sentinel Printing, Yarmouth


**Canadian Cataloguing in Publication Data**
Weier, John, 1949-

    Coils of the Yamuna

    ISBN 0-921411-59-6

1. India — Description and travel. 2. Weier, John, 1949- — Journeys — India. I. Title.

DS414.2.W44 1998      915.4      C98-950089-6


**Broken Jaw Press**
**MARITIMES ARTS PROJECTS PRODUCTIONS**
Box 596 Stn A
Fredericton NB E3B 5A6     ph/fax 506 454-5127
Canada               e-mail: jblades@nbnet.nb.ca

# *Coils of the Yamuna*

For Victor
for all your joy!
& for our shared past!
for the pleasure of
knowing you!

## John Weier

Broken Jaw Press

Fredericton • Canada

## Prologue

In the fall and early winter of 1994/95, my wife, Susan, and I made preparations for a journey to northern India. We visited travel agents and doctors. We read maps and pamphlets and diaries. We snapped photo portraits, applied for passports and visas, purchased tickets for air travel. We sent—and received in return—letters that we hoped would soften our arrival in this distant country: where should we spend our first night? which taxi should we take? what was a reasonable rate? how should we get to the hill-station, our initial objective? We shopped, and made lists of articles we would pack in our new luggage: money-belt, long underwear, normal underwear, toque, sandals, bird book, binoculars, insect repellant, chocolate bars ...

No amount of preparation for a journey can ever be enough. Like other travellers to foreign lands, we spent the last days before our departure with the anxiety that we'd forgotten some crucial matter, some article not packed, a telephone call not made. We worried about our medications, the timing of our visas, amounts of our traveller's cheques. We realized, suddenly, that we could never stay in India long enough. Some of our friends insisted that in our 21 days we would be foolish not to see all the various parts of India; surely we had plenty of time; or, they said, why bother going. Others suggested that in 21 days we could hardly see the sights of even one region, we should stay in one place, get to know at least a few Indian people. Of course, we had mortgages and jobs, obligations to consider; we couldn't just fly off and stay an extra 21 days.

I had been to India before; for several months in the mid-1970s, after studying eastern religions at university. I felt, upon graduation, that my education was incomplete, I needed to see another culture, see how unusual the world could be, I though India might change me in some dramatic way. A difficult journey, when are we ever complete?

An opportunity. My two teenage children from a previous marriage were spending a year in the Himalayan foothills with their new blended family, they would go to school there while their mother and stepfather taught. I couldn't bear the thought of being separated from them for such a long time. We decided to visit them, our children, stepchildren, at their school. We made our travel plans; we wanted to see a few of the other parts of India as well, and I had a chance to meet some Indian writers in Delhi. Susan had never been to India at all; nor anywhere in Africa, or Asia. How would she react? We talked about some of the difficulties we might encounter.

As on my first pilgrimage to India, I carried a notebook to record my reactions to the things I saw, heard, tasted. The vignettes that follow are based on those diaries, on our reading, on the letters from our children; a tapestry of our time spent in an enchanting kingdom.

I would like to thank the Manitoba Arts Council for its ongoing support. Thanks also to Douglas Reimer, Sean Virgo and Susan Stratford for their tireless work on the manuscript.

John Weier
Winnipeg
December, 1997

*For Anna, Jon and Susan*

*Travellers return from the city of Zirma with distinct memories: a blind black man shouting in the crowd, a lunatic teetering on a skyscraper's cornice, a girl walking with a puma on a leash. Actually many of the blind men who tap their canes on Zirma's cobblestones are black; in every skyscraper there is someone going mad; all lunatics spend hours on cornices; there is no puma that some girl does not raise, as a whim ...*

Italo Calvino, *Invisible Cities*

## February 3, 1995

The white-rumped sandpiper, they say—when it starts migration in July—departs the northern shores of Canada, tundra, follows the wind south and east across the Arctic, Hudson Bay, then flies from the Maritimes over the Atlantic to South America, not the shortest route, to the southern-most tip of South America, winters way down in Tierra del Fuego. That's a trip of 9000 miles, great hardship, at least one month in spring, two months in fall, feeding and resting and flying. The white-rumped sandpiper makes that trip, back and forth, 18,000 miles, to nest in northern Canada each new year.

How does it find its path? What impulse drives it? From the Arctic to Tierra del Fuego. All that way. I believe it's true, Peter Matthiessen says it's so. Sandpiper. White flash and tail, long wings. I can see it, I carry a memory map of the world inside my head. There. Flying up in August in Alaska. Settling again with its companions along the shores near Cape Horn a few months later. Why shouldn't I believe that? White-rumped sandpiper, wind bird, with its breast muscle, and quick metabolism, and hollow bone. The sandpiper is a bird of wonder and miracle, a bird with all the world as home.

Airport. Air traffic control. 747. Tomorrow my partner and I fly from Toronto halfway around the world to visit in India. East and west, north and south. India. How many miles is that? And how many hours, really? We'll leave here, fly for 24 hours, arrive there 36 hours later. Can you imagine, such peculiar obsessions with time? Far less prepared than the white-rumped sandpiper for our journey, yet so many of them never complete that first travelling cycle.

747. Basket of plastic and tin. It takes a certain kind of faith to keep *this* bird afloat, so high above the speeding ground. The sandpiper is a bird of wonder and miracle and great faith.

# India! Come discover India!
# Live like a Maharajah!

Explore this land of mystery, enchantment and romance. Wander through the caves, worship at the holy shrines, frolic on the golden beaches.

Begin your true Indian experience with a warm smile and *Namaste* welcome from a dark-haired and sari-clad hostess when you board an Air India 747 wide-bodied jet.

India offers everything a visitor might desire: palaces and temples, snow-capped mountains and lush tropical forests, rushing streams, lazy rivers, natural and manmade monuments, animals of every shape and size, birds of every colour, luxurious hotels, knowledgeable guides, modern trains, airplanes, motor cars.

Discover the wonder of India, now neatly packaged for you by Rama Tours.

**February 4, 1995**

Winnipeg to Toronto.

Air Canada. We've chosen to fly Air Canada, all the way to Delhi. I've been to India before. I know, seven, eight days from now, what that one word will mean: Canada. We'll pull our tickets from the briefcase. In bold letters. **Air Canada**. Canada, that one word for home.

Through the window of our aircraft I watch the cold runway. I see the hills of shovelled snow, shining snow, I shade my eyes. I see Winnipeg. Winter and sun and blue sky. See a body, standing, man or woman in a dark parka. Temperature, -21° Celsius. Susan settles into Row 12 beside me. On the other side of me a big red handle, a sign. Emergency exit.

That first trip to India 20 years ago never lost the feeling of emergency, of terror. The flight from Toronto to London was bumpy. Our aircraft slipped. Fell. Fell again. I thought I saw a bare wire under my seat. My hands gripped my armrests. I thought we would crash. I thought I would die before I ever tasted the Winnipeg winter again. All that first time I spent in India I thought about Canada. I thought I'd never see Canada again. I began to think of myself as Canadian. I told my friends after I got home that I became Canadian the morning I stepped off the plane in Calcutta.

I look back over the beginnings of my diary. Surprise. I notice that I've dated the first two entries in this journal "1994." By accident, of course, the new year. I can change that, stroke out my mistake, write '95 above. But will that help? Will that change anything? Suddenly I'm falling back in time. I've brought all my best clothes, my worst nightmares. Those two words: emergency, accident. I have lost everything already.

Susan turns to tell me how excited she feels about travelling to India. Says she's worried though about actually managing the flight, such a terribly long flight to India.

**February 4, 1995**

The religions of India: Hindu, Muslim, Sikh and Zoroastrian,
Buddhist, Jain. Those sacred rivers. Those dancing gods and
goddesses. A hundred golden temples. All the ancient literatures.

As a boy I knew little about Hindus, only what I learned from dark
and sombre white-skinned missionaries. Their talk, their slide shows.
That they had gone to India to make Christians out of Hindus. That
they dressed them in western clothes and gave them jobs as cooks
and drivers. That they splintered families. That they saved Hindus,
taught them how to pray. Hindus! Imagine! Teaching Hindus how to
pray! That was the only way to save them.

I grew up a Mennonite boy. Religion punched and poked into a
rucksack, what didn't fit we threw away, like burning old clothes. I
tried to keep myself hidden in a corner, I didn't want that Mennonite
God to notice me, nor anyone else. I never argued about it, heaven is
something we all wish for; but I couldn't believe that Hindus
wouldn't get to heaven on their own. I don't know where I got that
notion, I must have been inspired.

Later I developed a more serious interest in Hinduism. Even in high
school I'd understood already that my parent's faith was alien to me.
That did frighten me. Mahatma Gandhi, he was a man I admired.

## MANITOBA DEPARTMENT OF HEALTH
## TRAVEL MEDICINE ADVISORY: INDIA

**Languages:** Hindi and English

**Capital City:** New Delhi

**Population:** 910,000,000 (estimated)

**Area:** 1,269,000 square miles (⅓ the size of Canada)

**Annual Income Per Person:** 6,000 Rupees ($1 Cdn. equals R20)

**Climate:** India has only three seasons; cool, October to February; hot, March to June; and rainy, July to September. Only the mountainous areas have colder temperatures.

**Malaria** is transmitted throughout the country, even in urban areas, and cases of chloroquine-resistant plasmodium falciparum malaria have been confirmed. Travellers planning a visit anywhere in India are advised to use weekly mefloquine (lariam) prophylaxis.

**Diarrhea** is the most frequent health problem of travellers to developing countries. It is acquired through the ingestion of food and water contaminated with fecal material. Travellers are advised to follow food and water restrictions, especially when dining outside major hotels and resorts:
Drink only boiled or purified water
Drink canned or bottled beverages
Avoid ice cubes
Select food that is well-cooked and hot
Avoid salads
Avoid dairy products made from unpasteurized milk
Avoid food cooked at roadside stands

The risk of **rabies** infection is high in India. The pre-exposure rabies vaccine series is highly recommended for all persons. In the event of an animal bite, emergency medical care is required.

**Hepatitis B** infection is common among Indian inhabitants. The virus is transmitted by blood and other body fluids, contaminated intravenous equipment, tattoo needles, and through intimate or sexual contact.

Travellers are advised not to swim or bathe in rivers, streams, or lakes. The presence of unexpected pollutants, viruses, bacteria, or parasites may cause serious illness.

## Hindu Poet: 1

Have you seen the Buddha? Did you see how he stepped to
his mother's side? Did you see the seven suns, and the skin

of the moon, and the dark cloud? Have you seen the
Buddha? Can you catch that voice? Did he call in the night

to his father? Did he long for a daughter? Would he cry for
his wife and his son? Have you seen the Buddha? Did you

see the palace and the dancing women? Do you desire the
women? Did you dance with the women, did you mimic

those mad and dancing women, would you lie with those
women? And the old man? Have you seen the sick man,

the dead man by the road, the corpse in the grass? Did you
talk with your friends about the dead man, naked man,

corpse, the snake in the tall grass? Have you seen the
Buddha? And the forest? Did you see his frame and his fat,

the fig and the banyan tree? Did you watch with him for the
dusk, through the dark and the wet of the night? Did you

wait for the sun and the dawn? Have you ever seen the
Buddha? Did you hear him shout? Have you counted the

world, and the wheel? Have you seen the Buddha? Have
you seen the fire? Buddha fire, leaping flame, and the

bones, his bones, nothing left but a pile of white Buddha
bones. Have you seen the Buddha? If you ever chance to

meet the Buddha, if you're ever on the road and chance to
see the Buddha ... Ooooooooooooommmmmmmmmmm.

## February 4

Sick. What if we get sick in India? We've worried a lot about our
health as we prepared for India; in the last six weeks even our
television became obsessed with body, well-being. Travel in India
sounds like it constitutes a health hazard. We've heard stories.
Vomiting, diarrhea, three, four days; we should expect that. And so
far from our Winnipeg doctor, the nearest hospital. I remember how
it was the last time, when one of us got sick in Kathmandu. It took a
terrible week to recover.

We began the immunization two months ago:
> Four huge pills on alternate days for typhoid, my stomach
> churned and boiled and ached.
> Gamma globulin in the bum for hepatitis B. A thick serum, the
> nurse had trouble with the needle.
> A polio booster.
> And a shot for meningitis, the next day Susan couldn't lift her arms.
> I was lucky, I didn't need tetanus and diphtheria. I'd stepped on
> a rusty nail and got that shot two years ago.

We carry a bag of medical supplies:
> Doxycycline for malaria.
> Monistat cream for yeast infections caused by doxycycline, they
> tell us men don't get yeast infections but we know better.
> Imodium for diarrhea.
> Gastrolytes for dehydration because of diarrhea.
> Ranitidine for my duodenal ulcers, imitrex and naproxen to cure
> migraines, our Western diseases.
> Gravol tablets for travel sickness.
> The usual, and some unusual, contraceptives; their effectiveness
> reduced by all this medication.

We've brought a variety of skin creams; sunscreen with 45
protection, insect repellents. How do people ever stay alive in
foreign developing countries? Has anything changed since Alexander
the Great invaded India? Did Vasco da Gama suffer from malaria?

We travel with fear, memories of conversations in the
neighbourhood pharmacy, our medications are worth more than the
average Indian's annual salary.

**February 5, 1995**


Toronto to London.

I open my eyes. A swath of blue sky, stretch of orange and red, sunrise frames our aircraft window. Our small universe above, the curve of the earth's surface below, the home planet. You recognize the images from TV, nothing like the pictures from *Discovery*, but even this a wonder.

Morning. We've slept. Wake to hear the rattle of trolleys, breakfast dishes, to smell the morning coffee, eat croissant, scan the panel at the front of the cabin:
> *Altitude: 35,000 feet*
> *Ground Speed: 931 kph*
> *Tail Wind: 40 kph*

I remember reading that observers in small aircraft have clocked dunlins flying at 110 miles per hour. Pectoral sandpipers have been identified flying at 13,000 feet, bar-tailed godwits at 20,000 feet over the Himalayas. The American golden-plover travels more than 2,000 miles in a single non-stop flight. These birds have flown their old familiar routes for countless millennia. The sandpiper is a bird of wonder and miracle and great faith.

Awake, my arms and legs feel stiff, my head groggy, stomach a bit nauseous; even a walk up and down the aisle, back and forth, back and forth, doesn't help. Soon, I hope, we'll see the runway in England.

## February 5

Heathrow Airport, London.

About racism. Two things. Or maybe three or four.

Susan and I probably think like most middle class Westerners, we insist that we're not racist. We tell our friends that we believe all women and men are equal, deserve equal opportunities, that no one race stands higher than the other. But suddenly, at Heathrow, we face a departure lounge crowded with Indians. Foreign faces, foreign dress, foreign sounds, foreign colours and smells, a foreign crowd. Dark skins. An introduction to India. No *Namaste* and smiling *saried* hostess, this 747 will be full of real Indians. I see the surprise catalogued on Susan's face.

What do we feel? Anger? Fear? Isolation? All of those. Self-aware. White. We feel white. We look for other white faces. What did we think, that we were travelling to an India full of North Americans? If India is so poor, how can all these people afford to fly? We see suddenly that racism is not just a belief, but an emotion.

White faces. There. The airline staff, white too. They see us, pull us aside. They think they can give us an upgrade, put us in first-class. Is it because of my tie and jacket, because of Susan's modern skirt? Is it because of my smile, do they like my smile, smiles always look good in first-class. Probably they know that we're *Frequent Flyers*, that we fly Air Canada 12, 16 times each year; that must be the reason for the upgrade.

We do accept the airline's offer, step happily into first-class; big reclining chairs, lots of space, private TV, meals on white china, wine, hostess hovering with beverages and suggestions. Comfort. Luxury. We love our upgrade, our first-class accommodations.

Isn't this great, I say, as our plane leaves the runway. But my cheeks burn with shame, I know why we were chosen, I'm glad my writing colleagues in India can't see me here.

*... today I went to the bazaar for the first time. Except for all the men staring at me, it was great. I bought an umbrella and a notebook. I also bought a Canadian chocolate bar. There are tons of Canadian and American things here, things like coke and chips. Oh, there's also a really great shoemaker store. All you have to do is give them a tracing of your foot and a picture of the shoe you want, you pick out the leather, and they'll make you a shoe.*

*When we first came here I was really freaked out about bugs. Now, I don't mind any of the bugs except one, a certain kind of flying beetle. I've now hopefully gotten over my bug phobia.*

*Our house has one of the only two bathtubs here at Woodstock. On the day we moved in I came face to face with a poisonous scorpion in the bathroom. Don't worry Dad, it was poisonous, but not deadly.*

*Oh yeah, I was going to tell you. The other day we saw a rat in our kitchen. Gross! I kind of freaked out about that too. It's hard being here, sometimes I just cry because I want a Big Mac. I know that's silly.*

*Jon and I were going to call you yesterday but we don't know how to work our phone. Write soon!*

*Love*

**February 5**

London to Delhi.

Sometime in the evening the Big Dipper emerges in the north sky. And Polaris. Bright. I've never learned much about the stars, the planets; I can identify Venus and Mars; I've seen Hyakutake. I plot the few stars I know now while a voice on the intercom tells us that we've flown just north of Moscow. Even five years ago we would have taken a different route, would have travelled instead over Europe and Saudi Arabia, this would have been restricted Soviet airspace. The voice crackles on, informs us we're now over Kazakhstan, Uzbekistan, Afghanistan. All these alien distant places.

Through the window I follow the stretch of snow in the moonlight. And a long shining zigzag line far below us. Maybe a fence? Impossible. Maybe a road? Metal erectors and power lines? Maybe the trail used by Marco Polo when he rode from Samarkand.

This land, these words—Kazakhstan, Uzbekistan—pull at my memories. My father's stories. I gather images of Tatars and Huns, nomadic people, walking, riding on horseback, Mongolians, weathered faces and flocking sheep. Zhivago pictures of horse and sleigh and snowstorm. The vast Asian steppe. Ukraine. My parents youth, I know, 35,000 feet below me and a few days riding to the west.

The big screen on our 747 flashes our route, red arrow on a blue-green-brown likeness of the world. All the right topography but still the old rectangular world, already we are reaching for the eastern rim.

How dare we? Where do we think we're going? What will we do dropped into the heart of this strange continent, gawk at those Indian lives as though they were artifacts at any tourist's disposal?

## February 6, 1995

Wake at five this morning in New Delhi. A knock on the door and then the alarm. Stumble into the shower, cold; the long flight, the delays, last night still parading in my veins. We landed at midnight at the Delhi airport. Waited and waited for our luggage. Bumped ribs and elbows, jostled with the turban and Indian crowd, we clutched our handbags to our sides. Customs. Immigration. One hour, two. Dazed. We changed dollars to rupees, three traveller's cheques for a three-inch bundle of rupees. Six thousand, with an elastic band. I felt a hundred eyes on those bills. I stood at the money changer's kiosk and kept my head half-turned while Susan haggled with the taxi drivers. Here, this one. Susan called me, we were both shivering. Dark New Delhi streets to the YWCA, the clerk lay on the floor behind the counter, sleeping. He took our names. Yes, he was expecting us. We crawled into bed at three. Slept. Woke to the knock and the alarm at five.

By six we're back in the taxi, this one will take us the 300 kilometres to Mussoorie. I'm excited. Jon and Anna said they'd meet us at the school gate. Seven months since we saw them. Only seven hours to wait. All those worries about the mail, about their safety, almost over.

The Delhi streets still dark and quiet. We see bonfires in the downtown, men wrapped in shawls stand warming their hands. I remember the feeling of Calcutta 20 years ago. I felt such surprise when I arrived in Calcutta then, so many things that shocked me. Now the sun rises again in India. The first trees we see in the Delhi sun, naked and dusty, motionless against the sky. House crows gather with their gray capes. And vultures. And dark pariah kites. Buses belch black diesel smoke. Buildings sag and smudge and spin into rubble. We pass stale ponds; stacks of dung fuel patties; men, women squatting in fields and along the drainage ditches to empty their morning bowels. Our taxi rumbles through streets and traffic; from city, to town, to city, to village, to farm. A water buffalo pulls his wagonload of sugarcane, I can see right through his bones. That horse, with its cart, hobbling on three legs.

Just one small blemish of joy here on the Delhi to Dehra Dun highway—two-week-old buffalo calf kicks out its heels in the morning.

## Hindu Poet: 2

The five blind mendicant monks who wished to be introduced to an elephant, since childhood each of them has begged just once to see an elephant. Finally, one day, they hear rumours that an elephant waits at the square in the centre of the village. They approach. The first mendicant touches the elephant's trunk. He runs his hands up and down the elephant's trunk. Ah, he says. I see that an elephant is long

and stout. An elephant is strong, he says, but spineless. Finally, he says. Finally, now I can rest, now I've seen an elephant. The second mendicant monk bumps straight into the elephant's tusk. My, she says. (There must be women mendicants by now.) My, she says, she steps back. Look out. An elephant is long and hard, and sharp; elephants must be quite dangerous. Look out for the elephant, she says. Beware

the elephant. The third blind monk steps up and fondles the elephant's tail. An elephant is small like me, the third monk says. The third mendicant is still a child (in religious terms, at least). An elephant is short and thin, the third says. Short and thin. Hhhwew. And doesn't smell very good, the third monk says. The fourth mendicant monk strokes the elephant's ear. What a surprise, the fourth mendicant says.

I didn't expect this, an elephant is big and flat and floppy. Isn't this hilarious, he says. I find this elephant attractive, he says. In a flaccid kind of way, he says. An elephant is just like the naan my mother used to make for supper, he laughs. The fifth mendicant leans up against the elephant's side, she rests her head up against the elephant. (She's got an ear to the elephant's side.) She considers what the other blind monks

have said. Oh, says the fifth mendicant monk, she's the wise one. She hears a rumble deep in the elephant's side. Oh, that sounds like God, she says. She spreads her arms across the elephant's ribs. All this
reminds me of God, she says. She rubs to and fro along the elephant. She listens, she'd like to hear the elephant rumble again. God must be an elephant, she says. Ooooooooooooooooooommmmmmmmmmm.

**February 6**
**Guns**


Middle of the morning in the back of the taxi on the highway Susan turns to look at me.

Do you remember the policemen at the airport, she says. Do you remember their guns, they looked like machine guns, I guess they were machine guns. One of them, she says, told me which would be the cheapest taxi, he motioned toward me with his gun barrel. You were busy changing our money. How could I disagree with him. I was frightened. I called you. I didn't know where that taxi would take us.

**February 6, 1995**
**Road to Mussoorie**


Foreign script everywhere, on signs and buildings along the road. Curls and loops and lines hanging from a flat horizon. A secret Indian code. A traveller's conundrum. Notes to a treasure trove. Some English too. *Thums Up, The Great Refresher*; an ad for the native cola. *Madras Restourent*, Susan and I agree that it doesn't look clean enough for travelling Westerners. *Horn Please* stencilled on the back of every Indian truck, *At Night Use Dipper.* (*Use Dipper* we realize later refers to the Indian method of flicking a vehicle's bright beams. We never do understand that notice fully, it turns out many vehicles at night in India don't use any lights at all.)

*Horn Please!* Traffic here flows in a way you would never imagine at home in Winnipeg. Cars, trucks, and rickshaws. Bicycles and scooters. Jeeps. Carts and ponies. Water buffalo with their sugarcane loads. Tractors and pedestrians. All at their own individual speeds. They turn and twist and flow, around, beside, between each other as easily as rocks and river water.

The cars are all short and round ambassadors, the same ones I rode in on my last visit. Still the same body style, only the colour has changed, the old ones were black, all the new ones are painted the colour of eggshells.

What I noticed at the airport yesterday, I felt I had a much stronger sense of personal private space than the people around me. Maybe just a bigger space. My comrade travellers at the airport seemed quite content to bump my shins with their carts and suitcases, to elbow my delicate ribs, rub against my shoulders. I got annoyed at their lack of consideration. Even here on the highway today vehicles ache to rub bumpers, knead fenders. A two-lane highway is suddenly wide enough for four, five vehicles. Horns blare in mock greeting. Drivers of buses, lorries—we soon learn to call them lorries, as though we grew up in the middle of England—press gas pedals, promise rash and intimate encounters, then swerve aside last second, only inches from window to window.

The colour of eggshells. If rocks and river water had horns that they could blow.

# MUSSOORIE

Situated just 34 kilometres from Dehra Dun at an altitude of 2,126 metres (7,000 feet), Mussoorie offers a survey of the plains and the holy Ganga stretching to the south, the great Himalaya snow mountains silhouetted to the north. This 'Queen of the Hill Stations' was founded by the British Captain Young after he fell in love with the area while on a hunting expedition into the foothills in 1927. The first Mussoorie building constructed by Young has been converted into the Mullingar Hotel.

Mussoorie's proximity to the plains, its relief from the sweltering Indian heat, awesome view of the Himalayan ranges, and a wide variety of good accommodation, modern facilities, restaurants, entertainment centres, trek and picnic spots have transformed it into a year-round resort.

## February 6
## Mussoorie


And then the hills lurch from the plain in front of us. We drive up.
And up. Our taxi strains, whines. Switch
      back. Hair
      pin. Up, and up again. We meet lorries racing on the cliff edge,
swaying on the cliff edge. Our driver stops. Positions rocks carefully
behind each of our four wheels. Walks away from the car. Where is
he going? He kneels hard by the precipice. Scoops water from a
spring into his pail. Lifts the taxi hood. Pours water into the radiator.
Hiss and steam. He slams the hood again, climbs back into the car.
We drive on. One hour on the cliff edge, though it seems far longer,
we think only of those speeding lorries. Into the town of Mussoorie.

And music.

Radio clamours from a busy shop through our open car window.
Strings slide, and voices. Startled cadence and interval. Music jangles
      our nerves. Here
in the Mussoorie bazaar. One hundred small shops. The babel of
voices. Dark skin and hair. Every eye opens, every head turns, foot
stops. Everyone watches us, foreigners, passing in the taxi. Mussoorie
bazaar. The sight, smell, taste of it. Even taste. Through our open
window. Tongues rolling on our teeth and lips.

Honk, and roar, and ominous exhaust of taxi, lorry, mini-van. Clink
of cowbells when we stop, call of crows and mynas. One
      split
second silence and the call of a muezzin. A call to prayer, to some
imagined god and mosque and minaret. This single moan and
lamentation, this lonesome minaret, the mark of all that's foreign to
us here in India.

Then, suddenly again, a twist in the road, and Woodstock School. The
trees. The gate. There, Susan, there. Do you see them? Jon. Anna.
Two small children, grown. That last minute's wait to hold them.
The feel of them in my arms. Sound of their voices. Two of them.
Four of us. Circle of space and time. Suddenly, I feel at home again.

## Coolies: Susan

We hire coolies to carry our luggage up to Edgehill. Actually, Anna hires the coolies, she knows what to do. They strap our luggage to their backs and start up the hill. We climb on ahead.

I'm not sure what to think about the coolies but I have a nice feeling of being taken care of. I wonder about the coolies, they're smaller than me and they're carrying so much luggage. Do they eat enough food to carry such weights? I wonder about the origin of the word coolie, is it a kind word? Is 25 rupees a good price for carrying luggage up a hill?

## February 7

We rise at dawn to bird sound here in the hills of Mussoorie. These aren't the foothills of southern Alberta, calm and rolling. In Mussoorie, hills surge and fall, hills slash against other hills, ridges crash onto the plains.

We have taken a room at Edgehill, nine feet by fifteen, concrete walls and floor, sheet metal roof, nothing much to insulate us from the outside, food and lodging for a few dollars a night. Edgehill, just that, a guesthouse slung on the flank of a sharp incline. Other buildings sprinkle above, to the left, and right, but the rest, forest, blue southern sky and forest, tall green forest, the flatlands stretching below us.

Birds. We step outside with black binoculars in hand, new field guides purchased yesterday in the bazaar, Jon had marked them for us. Birds in the trees everywhere around us, a dozen species, more.

Red-headed tit, yellow-cheeked tit, green-backed tit, busy branch to branch, and chatter. Spotted gray creeper scrambling on a tree trunk. Indian white-eye flutters past. White-cheeked bulbul pair teeters on a hydro wire. Birds as bright as language, fresh as morning. Little scaly-bellied green woodpecker and lesser golden-backed woodpecker, both jackhammer high in the foliage. Streaked laughingthrush, blue whistling-thrush, orange-flanked bush-robin, all sulking in the weeds and brushes. A dozen blossom-headed parakeets fly far beneath us. For one hour we watch, and study, and point, then the birds are gone.

Susan and Anna and I crowd together for warmth just as a waiter and a gong parade in our narrow courtyard. Anna has spent the night in our room and leads us to breakfast. Cream of wheat, toast and jam, coffee.

We walk the trails east along the south face of the Edgehill ridge, the four of us. We touch trees, ferns, small yellow flowers on the rock face, we take photographs. A tawny eagle, there, drifting on the thermals. Mosses and lichens grow on tree stumps. We climb up, and north. Then west again, higher along the same rise. Our trail bends to the north side of the ridge. The trees change here, hidden from the sun, more pines and firs, snow scatters in crooks and crannies. We hear a scattering of birds. A gray tit, a yellow-fronted pied woodpecker, great Himalayan barbet. We stop to admire the snow peaks far in the distance. We point, somewhere out there in the northeast we imagine Everest.

We walk again, and lunch at a small shop in a village outside the gate to St. Paul's Anglican Church. A small church, Jon says there are holes in the church pews in front of you where you can rest your rifle while you worship, the days of British rule. And the graveyard too, stepped up into the hills on Camelback Road, all the names chiselled into the stones of British origin.

We walk again. This is Mussoorie; hiking, and forest, and birds. Nighttime we huddle round the heater in our room. Our one light bulb dims, and glows, and dims again. The taste of winter in the hills of northern India.

**February 8**

Our bodies stretch to find the shape of the Indian clock. Twelve hours torn from our Winnipeg schedule, at six in the evening our heads nod, we struggle against time, the need to sleep. Later, we sit upright in bed, eyes wide, we check the time, three in the morning.

Susan, beside me, is quiet. I know she's awake, wonder what she's thinking. She's cold; it's cold in our little concrete and sheet metal room in the middle of the night in the hills of northern India. She probably wishes she'd stayed at home in Winnipeg, wishes she'd never met me, never let me drag her into this adventure.

Our room has two single sagging wooden frame beds. Susan and I sleep in one; crowded, hard to roll over, but warm. Anna sleeps in the other. She's used to the cold, but congested, her breathing sounds thick and difficult. I have just enough time to worry about what's happened to her here in India; about Jon, his arms as thin as toothpicks, the food he tells me, and the exercise, up and down the hills—he lives in the dormitory a long walk down from us, dormitory food. Still their worrying father, then I tumble into sleep again.

## Small Bed: Susan

I tell John at breakfast that I *don't* wish I'd stayed at home; I *wish* I had a bit more space in the bed, such a tiny bed. And the way it sags in the middle, we roll down into each other. I say I feel caught between him and the wall.

Breakfast? French toast with cane syrup. Tea and coffee. Hot milk with a skin on top. The sugar comes in much bigger pieces than at home, opaque crystals, doesn't dissolve as easily.

Already our feet and legs feel sore from all the hill walking, always up or down. Our toes hurt from pushing against the ends of our shoes on the downhill.

**February 8, 1995**

After the waiter and the gong in the Edgehill courtyard in the early evening we all gather in the dining hall. Guests, some Woodstock School staff. We eat supper together; curry, egg malai masala, chola dal, naan. Bill, a Woodstock teacher, entertains us with stories about India.

Bill says he's from Indiana but he grew up in Egypt, Turkey, Vietnam, he's lived in many places. Lots of experience, he says, his parents were missionaries. He says India is a filthy place, Indians have filthy habits. He talks about garbage and uncleanliness, he complains about the water and the food. Bill says they've ruined the beaches, he says that Indians defecate on the beaches in Goa, they've ruined the beaches so Westerners no longer use them.

It's true in a way; we've seen a lot of refuse, rubbish. Plastic bags should never have been invented, they've all blown into the hills of Mussoorie, thousands of them; paper bags would have composted long ago. And we've imagined human feces on the hill trail. We've worried about cleanliness; Indian whites (towels or hankies) aren't as white as North American, nothing's as clean as home, nothing's as white as North America. But we're embarrassed by Bill's comments. And Winnipeg isn't always that clean either. What does Bill think? There's an Indian eating at our table, Indians prepare and serve our food, there are Indians all around us. Bill says that Christian Indians seem much cleaner than the others.

John, an Indian from Hyderabad, turns when he hears that I grew up a Mennonite, perhaps he needs to change the subject. He invites me to pray with him in his room on Wednesday nights while I'm at Edgehill, he's a Mennonite too he says. I feel sick, I don't know what to say, I'm going to look as bad as Bill, I gave up Mennonites and praying long ago.

## Hindu Poet: 3

Did you ever think what non-violence actually means? Do you remember Gandhi and his hundred thousand followers, in the movie, how they stood against the guns and the horses and the rushing soldiers? Sometimes even how they lay down, how the horses refused to step on them. Non-violence. A kind of harmless weapon of their own. In South Africa. In India. Fighting for reform. Without guns. They didn't want to take a life. Do you remember Gandhi? Do you remember all that? Have you read any of those books?

It's not just cows, you know. North Americans think it's the cows, the cows are sacred; North Americans laugh and shake their heads when they talk about the cows. But here's what I think. Americans can't even think that far, it's a failure of their imagination. It's not just cows. Every speck, and bit, and fleck, and spot of life in India is sacred. Indians believe that every shred of life is blessed and sacred. Are you American? Can you imagine that? Mr Thoreau would probably have understood that.

You see those monks on the sidewalk, naked except for the one careful cloth at their waist, the piece of rag they clutch over their mouths. Holy men. Sweepers swing and sway around them with their feathered brooms. Those monks don't want to step on any living thing, they don't want to kill even an insect by breathing it. Non-violence. Did you ever think what that actually means? Many many Indians never eat meat. When you visit in India you will likely be a tourist vegetarian.

Every spot and bit of life is sacred. You should think about this the next time you slap a mosquito. You could think about it next time the crop duster flies over your house, next time you pass the abattoir on Marion Avenue, if you hear a scream and smell the frightened bloody cattle. Did you ever think how much you depend on the life around you? Did you ever think of this while eating carrots? Even vegetables were once alive.

Ooooooooooooooooooooooooooooooommmmmmmmmmmmmmmmmmmmmm.

## AN ACCOUNT OF THE TRAVELS OF MARCO POLO AS DICTATED TO RUSTICELLO OF PISA IN A GENOA PRISON, 1298

About 60 miles to the west of Ceylon lies the province of Maabar which is part of Greater India. This is the most beautiful place in India, the noblest and richest in all the world, and is divided between five kings who are brothers. Because of the temperate climate the citizens wear nothing but a loincloth in winter and summer alike, and no tailors whatsoever dwell throughout the whole of Maabar. It is never too hot or too cold. The king walks about as naked as everyone else but his loincloth is woven of rich material and he wears a necklace studded with rubies, sapphires, emeralds and other stones. Round his neck, and hanging down over his chest, he carries a narrow silk cord threaded with 104 pearls. That number of pearls because every day, morning and night, the king prays to his idols and repeats the prayer *Pacauta, Pacauta, Pacauta* 104 times. Round each arm the king wears three gold bracelets encrusted with precious stones and large rare pearls. He wears three gold bands set with jewels and pearls around each leg, and even more jewels on his feet. Every year the king issues a proclamation inviting any subject to bring pearls or precious stones to the court where he will be paid twice their value for them.

The king gathers a large following of the 'faithful' around him. These faithful believe that they serve the king not only in this world but in the next as well. They wait on the king, ride with him, and have a great deal of authority throughout the kingdom. When the king dies, his body is burnt and the faithful throw themselves on the funeral pyre and burn with him, so as to accompany him to the next world.

In this kingdom everyone, including the king and his suite, sits on the ground. If they are asked why they do not sit in a more dignified manner, they reply that it's extremely dignified to sit on the ground. We ourselves, they say, are made of earth and are destined to return to earth, so the earth can never be too highly respected and should not be held in contempt.

February 8
**Mussoorie Bazaar**


Mussoorie bull wanders the narrow streets of the bazaar. He stands.
He dozes. Wakes again. Snuffles through garbage. Eats
broccoli. Catches up with a cow in front of the theatre. Sniffs
at her bum. When you first see him in the street in front of
you, you wonder if you should run, hide, bulls must be
dangerous. Then you see that he's lame, left rear hock
swollen, you feel a bit safer.

A tangle of hydro and telephone wires, clotheslines and fluttering
laundry. No wonder my phone/fax calls from Winnipeg get
lost. They crisscross the market, zip to that balcony, the
stone patio, the pole. They choose the wrong wire, how
should they know. One good windstorm here would
probably send broken wires in every direction, lots of people
would die, if the power was on. There, a white mesh satellite
dish leans from that hot tin roof.

Common mynas, pied mynas, brahminy mynas, Indian equivalents of
our European starlings. Indian jungle crows. Pariah kites.
These clamber and caw and caper on the roofs, in the sky,
through the trees.

Industry. Indians work hard for their living. Ten by ten foot shops
crowd the bazaar. Shoemakers, tailors, grocers, jewellers,
restaurateurs, lumber dealers, furniture builders.
Shopkeepers work, wait, work. Porters, small, Tibetan-
looking, stagger under their 60 kilo loads.

One group of young men and boys plays cricket at the intersection
near the clock tower. The bowler. The ball. The swinging
bat. The ball squirts into one of the shops. A fielder follows,
crawls under a wooden bench reaching for his prize. I watch.
I wave and laugh. They laugh back. I snap a picture, their
faces turned and smiling at me.

Bulls in India don't seem as angry as bulls on North American TV.
Mussoorie bull still does his job, even though he's lame,
even though he's not angry. Everyone knows him. Everyone
jokes about him. Mussoorie bull, he sniffs at a cow in front
of the theatre.

The men in Mussoorie stare at Anna and Susan. And I've caught a
few Mussoorie women looking at me. Their eyes seem
pointed, intent. What are they thinking? What do they see?

Dear Susan and Dad,                                    16.9.94

How are you? I'm doing all right in India.
Things are a bit tense in Uttar Pradesh at the
moment though. For the past 4 weeks people
have been protesting for a separate state,
Uttarakhand, here in the mountainous region.
The protests were peaceful at first. Then, last
week, 9 people were killed in a clash with police
in the bazaar in Mussoorie. That was bad
enough. Yesterday, a bus drove off the edge of
a cliff on the road from Dehra Dun, 22 people
died. The medical staff from school hurried to
the local hospital to help with the injured.

You've probably read about the pneumonic
plague in the newspaper. That seems to be a real
problem in the plains, but shouldn't affect us
here in the hills. Don't worry. Mussoorie is tense
and under curfew because of the police violence,
but we are fine here at the school. Don't worry
about Anna, she's safe too.

In two weeks quarter break starts. We will
go hiking at Manali farther into the Himalayas.
Today is my 68th day away from home. I've
written 42 letters and have written Susan's
grandmother at least once. I've received eight
letters from home and hope for more soon. I
love hearing from home. I wear the necklace you
gave me for Christmas everyday. I also wear my
Goldeyes cap a lot.

Love

## February 9

Monkeys thrive in Mussoorie. Rhesus monkeys stroll, sit, watch and mate along the top of the stone wall in the Mussoorie bazaar. Langur monkeys wait in the branches high above the forest floor. Jon says we shouldn't look them in the eye, especially the langurs, they might see that as aggression, they might attack. He says the rhesus monkeys wake him every morning in the dorm. They swing from the trees through the early sun and mist, they crash on the sheet metal roof, gallop across, vanish in the trees at the far end of the building. He falls asleep again. Ten minutes. Then they're back. Crash. Gallop. Anna says the langur monkeys are lazy, sometimes they'll pee on you from up in a tree.

Monkeys with their mates and families and babies scatter all along the forest roads to Rishikesh. A story is told in the ancient literature of the god Hanuman who brought his monkey hosts to help the prince, Rama, in his battle against the evil Ravana. Millions of monkeys, they formed a long monkey bridge.

The road to Rishikesh. Traffic. I tell Anna that I'm surprised never to see people hurt on the Indian highways, there's so much traffic. She says I should just wait. She says that it happens. She says that if you hit someone with your car on the highway, a pedestrian, that you keep going, don't dare stop. You drive for your life. She says probably relatives of the injured or dead pedestrian will wish to kill you. You must remember to hit and run, you better just run, she says.

Jon says the Beatles visited in Rishikesh in the 1960s, dropped from the sky in their helicopter, much too far to drive; he says he heard that somewhere, they came to meet some famous yogi.

## February 9

The way the traffic jams and flows, mingles on the highway to
    Rishikesh. Motors and horns and hooves, bells and brakes
    and voices, dogs and crows, clattering carts. Clamour,
    cacophony. Dust and exhaust.

The way the branches of banyan trees drop roots. Twisting, curling,
    hanging roots. Banyan trunks falling from the sky. And their
    bark, smooth skin, almost human trunks. Large and
    spreading banyan tree, big as a city block. I love trees.

The deep wine-coloured robes of the Tibetan Buddhist monks—our
    driver says they're Tibetan. And the orange robes of the
    other monks. Their naked brown monk heads, the way their
    faces wrinkle and smile. They look calm, tranquil, like
    monks should. The traffic doesn't bother them.

The saris of wealthy Indian women. Red, orange, gold, blue, green,
    maroon; print and splash of colour, so many bright colours.
    The babel and bangle of all their jewelry. The careful
    turbans of Mr Man Mohan Singh Jaiswal, our taxi driver.

The way cattle, elephants, monkeys, Shivas, Krishnas, Mahatma
    Gandhis, carve in sandalwood. Thin and hungry Buddhas.
    Fat, laughing Buddhas. Breathe in! The warm smell of
    sandalwood.

That new and shiny Massey Ferguson 255 tractor in that last village.
    One young man in the seat, another on each fender. The way
    that load of sugarcane obeys the tractor.

All the goats in India. They've grown so fat. The nannies' swollen
    sweating teats. White and brown and black goats. Those goat
    kids look like you should take them home.

The way the bridges sway when we cross over the Ganga at
Rishikesh, the tickle in our stomachs. The beautiful
turquoise blue of the water. The shimmer and wings of the
plain sand martin. The way the river curves from the base of
the mountain, the home of Rsi Raibhya.

## Beggars: Susan

I notice the beggars. Small dark-eyed girls begging on the swinging bridge across the Ganga. They come and beg from John, they ignore me. The man, the head of the family, he's supposed to carry all the money. I notice how they look at him, how they hold out their hands to him, block and bother him, how annoyed he gets. No end to teenage begging girls in Rishikesh. This once I feel lucky to be a woman.

I notice the flowers, all the flowers in the temples as we walk up the lane, offerings to the gods. I point at the brightly coloured pictures of Krishna and Shiva. I notice the river, clear and blue, people walking on the sand and bathing in the holy river.

**February 9**

And then we leave Rishikesh—leave the ashrams, and the monks, and the Ganga—and drive back to our home, back up the one-hour cliff, back to Mussoorie and Edgehill for supper. We walk from the Woodstock School gates back up the hill to our room. Home, so easy to call it that with the kids living here. Is that how it is once you have children, their home also yours, wherever they make it?

The food at Edgehill: Curry, dahl, paratha, chapatti, papadhum, curd, naan, paneer, kabuli, gobhi, biranyi, bhaji, loki. Lentil dishes and chick peas and rice. A variety of breads, some of them stuffed with potatoes or cauliflower. Oh, what wonderful and unusual breads, we love the naan especially. Porridge or cream of wheat for breakfast, British leftovers. French toast or pancakes, with Indian sugarcane syrup. Custard desserts. Peppers and spice and variety. Vegetarian. Anna says the food is much better here than down below at the school, at the dormitory where Jon eats.

We watch how the waiters hover behind us, linger for a moment over our shoulders. More rice? More curry? More coffee? They offer baskets of fruit; banana, apple, mango. We eat. We visit. Now and again the cook marches between the tables. We find pleasure in the food at our home in Edgehill, we wouldn't once trade for bacon or steak or hamburger.

## THE GREAT NAVIGATOR: VASCO DA GAMA; HIS TRAVELS, DOMINIONS & NAVIGATION,
(*Sail The Indian Sea*, Vincent Jones)


At noon, at the turn of the hour-glass, a gun fired in the flagship. At once from the yards of the inshore vessels thirty-four prisoners were hanged by the neck—a sight which drew to the beach a multitude of people weeping, shouting and cursing. Another gun signal brought a cannonade from the whole fleet, catching all these people in the open. A few shots answered; but the Calicut guns had little power and were worked with little skill. Throughout the remainder of the day the ship's guns played on the city.

At nightfall the hanging bodies were hauled down. Their feet, hands and heads were cut off. The mutilated carcasses were thrown into the sea to float ashore. Feet, hands and heads were piled in a canoe. With them, set at the top of a lance, was a large notice written in the vernacular. The admiral (Vasco da Gama) ordered a cease-fire so that when this fine sight reached the shore no one should be kept away from seeing it.

**February 10**

Evening.

After six days in India I already feel restless for the comforts of
Canada. My bed. My furnace. The hot water tank. The bath. The
fridge. Old friends. My sense of adventure seems to stop at this, I
would like to spend every night at home in my own bed. I feel a bit
like my own son, writing:

> *Today is my 68th day away from home. I've written*
> *42 letters ... received eight letters from home, I love*
> *hearing from home.*

Did you weigh the yearning in those three simple numbers? Like
most westerners I am committed to the idea of travel, but tonight I
find such a gap between the idea and the travel itself.

I become nervous and irritable, crazy. Susan and I with one of our
grown children every night in this small room. No TV or VCR to
hypnotize us, nothing but a single deck of cards, nowhere to go. I'd
like to crash the walls out.

Wind claps on our sheet metal roof. The sky hangs heavy with cloud.
Leaves whisper. These Himalayan oaks speak much the same
language as the elm trees on Ashburn Street. They gossip about rain.

## Hindu Poet: 4

I love you
I love you in the flowers
I love you in the rose, love you in the tulips and the poppy, love you
     in the fuchsia, the cactus
I love you in the gray tit and the bush-robin, the creeper
I love you in the tiger and the langur
Love you in the stars, in the moon, in the rain and in the cold
I love you in the weather
Yes, I love you in oranges, and in mangos, and in curry, love you
     even in the rice
Love you in the moss and rocks
Love you on the cliff and in the cave
Love you in the brown, in the green
Love you in the wood and in the water, in the water buffalo
I love you in the minute, in *a* minute, love you in the year
Love you in the dawn, in the daytime, in the breath and in the life
     and in the light
I love you in the blade and in the bridle
I love you in the pine and in the pyre
I love you in the drum and the violin, the sitar and harmonium, in the
     trumpet and the bass
I love you in the bow and in the arrow
Love you in the bee and in the bean
In the soup and in the honey
Love you in your breasts
Love you in your thighs, in your eyebrows and your eyes, I love you
     in your sex
Love you in your lips and in your skin
Yes, I love you, and I love you, and I love you
Oooooooooooooommmmmmmmm.

## February 11

Rain, rain, rain. Everybody at breakfast talks about the winter monsoon.

It started raining in the middle of the night. Now, at noon, it's still pouring. We're trapped in this room, concrete floor and walls. The rain bangs and thunders on our metal roof.

Rain, rain, rain.

The hydro's off again, no lights, and our candles have burned right down to the holder. Cold, we can't even plug in the small heater we rented, temperature maybe 8 Celsius. We run next door to the dining room and borrow a few green candles we noticed there earlier, desperate for even that bit of heat. The romance of living in nature, in tents, roughing it; something I've never been good at.

Rain, rain, rain. Freezing cold. Why did we come here?

Maybe this rain will replenish the water and hydro supplies, Anna says it might, our water was turned off yesterday. We sit and wait. Anna, Susan and I. Play cards. Jon with his buddies waits somewhere below in the dorm. I teach Anna and Susan, finally, how to play *Hearts*; never enough time at home in Winnipeg. I teach them too well, they beat me again and again. Anna says she's glad it's not summer monsoon. In summer monsoon everything in her room grew mould. She says the forests, though, burst with flowers.

Rain, rain, rain. Winter monsoon.

We check the light. The power's come on, but so weak our 100 watt bulb barely glimmers. Our red-coiled heater gives up an illusion of warmth. We sit all day huddled in our room. We wear lots of clothes; longjohns, pants, four or five tops, two pairs of socks. We drape wool blankets around our shoulders, look like three bewildered bedouins.

Rain, rain, rain.

**February 12, 1995**

This morning's hike to Witch's Hill has to be abandoned. Witch's Hill, or Fairy Hill, so-called because of the ore deposits and the high incidence of lightning strikes, electrical discharge. You can see the lightning spark from up at Edgehill. Our goal here at Mussoorie, to trek the hill and forest trails, frustrated by the weather.

Beautiful morning walking, suddenly we step into a dense cloud. We watch it come, from below, watch it spin and swirl, watch the rain slash toward us. We lift our umbrellas, we hurry back, a good half-hour back up the trail to Edgehill. By the time we get there we're completely soaked. Our cold damp room. No light. No heat. No water. When the water's on Edgehill staff bring us a bucket of hot water every morning for our shower, today especially we miss the hot water.

Winter monsoon. Goddamned monsoon. Clouds roll by the door of our room, lunge straight from the plains. Clouds crash around buildings and hills. Fog turns to drizzle, turns to rain, turns to crackling and hail, back to clouds again. Another kind of beauty.

Anna sits with us again in our room. Jon's older, he's walked back down to the dorm, to spend time with his teenage friends.

We play *Hearts* again. We've lost two days of trekking because of weather, can only imagine what we might have seen on the trail to Witch's Hill, have to settle for Anna's stories.

Hi Dad and Susan,                                    21.10.94

    We started out on Saturday at five o'clock,
about 24 of us in a bus the school had rented.
First we drove from Mussoorie to Dehra Dun. At
Dun our four bus drivers wanted to stop for
supper. We waited because we had already
eaten. My friend, Annie, and I made faces at a
group of men, they seemed so enamoured by our
blonde hair. We had arranged with the drivers
to drive all night to Manali but at three o'clock
they stopped. They said they needed to sleep.
We asked why one couldn't drive while the
others slept; that's how we found out we only
had one driver, the others were hitching a ride.
In Manali we did all the tourist things; shopped
in the bazaar, visited temples, drove up into the
highest vehicular mountain pass in the world, got
dysentery... Kidding. We watched some old
hippies get stoned. We saw lots of hippies in
Manali, there's supposed to be a good supply of
cheap marijuana. The bus trip back was the real
adventure. We had to wake the drivers at five in
the morning. They kept pestering us for more
money (the trip had been prepaid). We found out
there'd been a riot in Dehra Dun, now there was
a curfew so we couldn't drive through at night.
We stopped at a guesthouse where we were told
to be careful of cobras. In the morning, when we
woke up, our bus was gone, the drivers had left
without us. We had to rent another bus. We
drove to Mussoorie the back way. What an
adventure!

Love

## February 12


The mountains around Mussoorie humble and excite you with their
   beauty. Trails trace the life of each hill and valley, side to
   side, up to down, through rock and forest. Some inspired
   environmentalist has tagged a variety of trees; western
   yellow pine, Himalayan cedar, rhododendron, Atlantic cedar.
   Atlantic cedar, how did that get here? I take pleasure in his/
   her forethought, I wish I knew more about trees, find the
   western yellow pine especially beautiful. Long needles.
   Coarse scaled bark.

We find eyesores along the trail; garbage dumped in the gullies, red
   and white and blue plastic rustling among the trees. I still
   feel confused and upset about this, about Bill and his Indian
   garbage, since Bill I feel guilty every time I notice garbage, I
   feel that as a visitor I shouldn't notice. I hate to see garbage
   in the forest, even in Canada.

We meet Indians; four men with pick and shovel and mortar to repair
   the trail, a woman gathering brush for firewood. We meet
   donkeys carrying loads, and a driver, many of the
   households in this region receive their deliveries on donkeys.
   One Jersey-coloured cow feeds and gongs on the hillside.

They say that during summer monsoon this forest fills with wild
   flowers, that orchids hang from every tree. Wish we could
   have seen that.

## February 13

Sun again. Susan and I hurry from our room in the morning and into the courtyard. We search out small spots of sun that we can wallow in, relish the way the sun heats our bodies.

We meet an American couple at breakfast, they have been working in Afghanistan since 1973, he's an optometrist. They tell us how terrible the situation is in Afghanistan, especially for women, how insignificant they are, how sometimes they're left to die. The couple has dropped off their daughter for school, Woodstock School starts back tomorrow, second term, Jon and Anna are getting ready too.

After breakfast Susan and I walk along the road east toward Flag Hill. Supposed to be a Buddhist place with prayer flags, this road's supposed to lead to Flag Hill but we can't find it. We see women washing their laundry and laying it to dry on large rocks in the sun. We see buildings in the valleys on either side, ruins, but no prayer flags. We should have been more careful about directions, written them down. We meet a group of men along the road walking from the east. We ask them. Flag Hill? Buddha? They speak no English, don't understand my hand signs. Jon tells us later that Flag Hill is never very easy to find.

A canvas-backed jeep roars over a rise in the road in front of us. We step aside to let it pass, I smile and wave hello. The jeep putts and squeals to a stop. A dozen Indians shuffle to make room for two travellers, they've misread our hello. The jeep putts off again. We wave goodbye. One gesture. One word. Meanings twist and turn in a foreign country, Indians often shake their heads *no* while they say *yes*.

After a mile or two on the road, Susan points to a trail north along the hillside. I ask her just how many thousand years she thinks people have walked this trail. We pass through forests of pine and rhododendron. Examine moss, lichens, ferns, sand. Small white-petalled flowers bloom under our feet. We stop to eat the lunch I carry in our knapsack while blossom-headed parakeets shriek in the treetops.

**February 13**

No power. No running water. Today we bought a pair of green candles in the bazaar and returned them to the dining room. I sit in the room in the evening and make these notes by candlelight. Our last day in Mussoorie. We'll go to bed early. We've said goodbye to the children. We've hired Mr Man Mohan Singh, the driver, to take us on a sightseeing tour, we leave for Agra at four in the morning.

Anna's bed stands empty, our room tonight far too big.

## Hindu Poet: 5

Having read pages and pages of the ancient literature; the Puranas,
    Mahabharata, Yoga-sutras;
Having read about the terror brought by powerful rajas; about deceit
    and greed and dissension; about varieties of evil omens,
    calves not sucking, cows not giving milk, horses weeping,
    images of gods and goddesses sweating from fear;
Having read about killing and war, oceans and mountains, swords
    and horses and chariots, wealth and golden bracelets and
    earrings; about Krishna's sixteen thousand wives;
Having read about ritual and sacrifice, about spider and snake bite,
    about the holy waters of the ganga, about singing birds and
    bright flowers, lust and playfulness;
About the mango and the apple; about nature and time; about sky
    and earth and fire;
Having read about elements and elephants; about long hair and
    navels; about sun and moon and metamorphosis;
Having read about incarnations; about incantations; about holy men,
    their dreams and prayers and devotion; about monkey-gods
    and elephant-gods; about the black and angry goddess;
It still all sounds so foreign to me. I haven't found one mention of
    weather. Not one word about the cold in the hills in winter.
    Not even a hint about the summer heat. Not one rune about
    the rhythm of the rain, the moment of the monsoon,
    momentum of the monsoon.
Ooooooooooooooooooooommmmmmmmmmm.

## February 14

Valentine's Day.

4 a.m. The Mussoorie bazaar lies empty. Rained hard all night, stopped just long enough for us to carry our luggage the quarter mile downhill to the hospital, one of the Edgehill kitchen staff woke up early to help us. Dark. Susan and I hand over hand along the trail and the railing. We've hired this car and Mr Singh to take us to Agra, to the bird sanctuary at Bharatpur, on to Jaipur and Delhi. Six days. Mr Singh talks and talks as we twist down the hill toward Dehra Dun. He insists he doesn't want our money, just the honour of taking us on our journey. He talks about respect and about pleasing his customers. He talks while we think about his R7,000 fee.

Seven thousand is a big number, it's the *thousand* that catches in your throat. We did think about haggling, everybody says we should do that in India, but how can we learn so quickly. And it's cheap enough when we convert to Canadian, we often forget that in India, to convert to Canadian. A $50 day, for a car, gas, a driver and guide.

We notice orchards along the road. Mango and guava, Mr Singh says. The trees look fresh and green, well kept, as good as any orchards in Canada. We pass acres of sugarcane, tall and reaching sugarcane, lots of fields of mustard, a few of wheat.

A crowd gathers suddenly as we drive through the city of Meerut. Trouble. Men. They look angry. They wave their arms. There, a roadblock. Mr Singh shouts through his open window. One man in the crowd turns and answers. A bus pulls in behind us, more angry men. Mr Singh spins the car. Stops. Accelerates. Spins again. Accelerates. We break free of the crowd. Circle the bus. We escape. Protest, Mr Singh says, political trouble, two people have been killed by the police at the university. We must leave before the police come again, he says. Just another $50 day for Mr Singh.

We travel south. We see lots of birds, though we can't name them, we'd have to stop to get a better look. We spot vultures. And vultures. And vultures. Thousands of them. Indian white-backed vultures, we check our field guides. We pass at least a half-dozen accidents, lorries smashed and scattered along the pavement. A driver lies on a mat beside his shattered cab; he looks injured, but no one stops to help him.

Susan and I, in the back seat of the taxi, hold each other's hands. We feel suddenly how our children protected us in Mussoorie, they are already seasoned travellers in India. We feel grateful for the presence of Mr Singh.

## Rupees: Susan

The rupee notes that we carry look worn and dirty. They have an unusual feel between our fingers, waxy, oily, they don't feel like paper anymore. Indian shopkeepers don't like to take the old or torn ones.

When we buy them in the bank they come stapled in fat bundles, rupee notes with staple holes everywhere. We have to show our passports and sign a series of papers. We're told we shouldn't take rupees out of the country.

In the banks, guards with machine guns wait in the halls and corners.

# AGRA

One of the oldest cities in India, Agra grew into prominence as the capital of an empire that spread across most of Afghanistan and India. This 16th and 17th century Mughal kingdom was ruled by the famous emperors Babar, Akbar, Shah Jahan, descendants of the great Genghis Khan. Akbar, especially, governed with great wisdom and tolerance.

Discover the architectural marvels of that ancient kingdom; the Taj Mahal, the sandstone Agra Fort. Discover the dazzling creations of Agra's modern craftsmen; leather goods, carpets, inlaid marble, jewelry.

Visit Fatehpur Sikri, the deserted city, Akbar's capital-to-be, where phantoms of ancient pomp and splendour still witness to his vanished dream.

Rich cream and curd sauces, succulent kebabs, fermented flour naan, tandoori parathas roasted in earthen ovens; Agra restaurants specialize in this excellent Mughlai cuisine.

## February 14

Fourteen hours driving, straight south, the afternoon sun hot through our car window. I tell Susan about the Taj Mahal and Agra. I tell stories about my first visit; how we stayed in the home of a retired Sikh general, how the rats ran across our bed, how we rode to the Taj on bicycle rickshaws, how the peddlers hounded us. Finally we arrive.

We weave through ancient and narrow streets to find the red Agra Fort. Mr Singh says he'll wait for us outside. Hawkers cluster round us on the sidewalk; they offer wooden carvings, chess sets, inlaid soapstone boxes, pocket-sized elephants, postcards, tours of the fort. I wave them away with one arm. Indian entrepreneurs are used to working hard to earn their living; they clamour, and push, and badger, bump against us, we can hardly walk. Susan, I know, is frightened. I get angry. I shout at them, and wave my arm again, but they persist until at last we step through the gates of the fort.

This Mughal emperor, Akbar, became famous as a builder, his Agra Fort grows and grows around us, massive red stone. Arches, columns, towers, vaults, spires; stunning workmanship but in terrible repair. I wish for some trace of Jon and Anna, here on their winter break less than a month ago, half the tour-bus got sick. We wander through buildings, up staircases, beside pools and gardens. A young European woman in a thin shift walks just ahead of us, she and her partner, I watch the shadow of her limbs, her breasts through cloth. We follow them, climb, step suddenly onto a small verandah. There, beyond the coils of the Yamuna, the Taj Mahal sparkles in the sunlight.

Romance. Tonight. One single opportunity for us to see the Taj Mahal by full moon on the day of Saint Valentine. But Susan and I are far too tired, and our hotel offers running water, a real shower; we plan instead to eat supper in the hotel's dining room.

## February 15, 1995


The contradictions of ugliness and beauty, poverty and wealth. The
Taj Mahal; its garden, flowers, green trees, ponds; its birds,
rose-ringed parakeet and Indian roller; its white marble
dome and sunrise, mountains of rock inlaid in semi-precious
stone; its gates and minarets. But just outside those gates, the
dogs and beggars, their maimed bodies.

The Yamuna River behind the Taj lies stagnant and dirty, banks litter
with garbage, swarm with varieties of vultures and kites and
crows. Still, two painted storks dabble knee-deep in the
water, sandpipers race on the mud flat, black-winged stilts
stretch their awkward legs. Ruddy shelducks float and preen.
Egrets flap and sail, flap and sail.

Shah Jahan, what does that name inspire? This tomb took 20 years
and 20,000 men to build. And one favourite wife. I have
checked the calculations of Sam Clemens on his world tour,
and I've spoken to his Satan.

Order. Balance. Symmetry. Matching ponds and minarets. Two
bodies, man and woman, lovers. Perfect squares and circles
crumbling, tumbling into turmoil.

I think it's the threat of anarchy that frightens me. In the stones and
in the buildings. On the highway. In the market. Caught in
that angry crowd in Meerut. Demons of death and disorder
steal the arms, legs, bodies, lives of Indian animals and
people.

Hi you guys, 3.11.94

Today is Diwali. Diwali is a Hindu festival sort of like Christmas. It celebrates the ancient victory of Rama, the Prince of Ayodhya, over the demon-king Ravana. Ravana had kidnapped Rama's wife, Sita. When Rama and Sita returned home to Ayodhya, they found the whole city bright with lights to welcome them. During Diwali people string lights in the bazaar, everyone buys fireworks.

I was looking forward to seeing the bazaar. Now though, I'm not going, there is a threat of violence again. Some local leaders have asked Mussoorie not to celebrate because of the separation killings. Still, I can hear the fireworks popping this very minute. Holy cow! That was a loud one. I hope this doesn't keep up all night, I do need some sleep.

Tomorrow we're going to the bazaar to pick up a dress we had made for me at the tailor's.

Love

## February 15

Craftsmen,
and women, it's true, dazzling
creations. So many
people here still working
with their hands.

A treadle sanding wheel; an orange slip
of stone chased into a petal. Warp and weft,
wool and shuttle. Chisel, graver, handsaw
and file. Knife, awl, hammer.
Fire. Tong and plier. Paint
and brush. One long bolt of quiet
cloth, a wooden block design, kitchen
saucer full of dye; one young man
at work, dip and stamp.

Craftsmen, craftswomen, the beauty
of their hands and eyes, their work.

Marble box, Sahib? Handmade
silk, Sahib? One
green carpet, Sahib? What
would you like, Sahib? Would you like
to buy, Sahib?

But we haven't come to buy. We came
to see, to visit, learn. We fear
that India will hate
us for our careful
habits. We are, after all, rich
Westerners.

## February 15


We're almost home.

Except for the big gates, the walls, palaces.
Except for the turrets and domes, the balconies;
        the treasury building,
        the armoury and banquet hall.
Except for the acres and acres of carved stone.
Except for the chambers and hidden corridors for Akbar's one
thousand women.
Except for red flowers, bougainvillea,
        for the hot sun in February.
Except for the Indian chat, brown bird that calls from perch to perch;
        the bright saried and suited young women from some
        Madras girl's school picnicking on the lawn.

Fatehpur Sikri.
Deserted city.
City of dry wells.
City without water, Akbar's affront.
Balanced on a green hill above the plain.

I feel drawn to this place.
From here I can see far into the future.
From here everything looks like prairie;
        everything looks like prairie and home.

---

## FORMULA FOR THE TREATMENT OF DIARRHEAL DISEASE

Prepare two separate glasses with the following:

Glass Number 1

| | |
|---|---|
| orange, apple or other fruit juice (rich in potassium) | 8 ounces |
| honey or corn syrup (glucose) | 1/2 tsp |
| table salt (contains sodium and chloride) | 1 pinch |

Glass Number 2

| | |
|---|---|
| carbonated or boiled water | 8 ounces |
| baking soda (sodium bicarbonate) | 1/4 tsp |

Drink alternately from each glass until thirst is quenched. Supplement as desired with carbonated beverages, boiled water, or scalding tea. Avoid solid foods and milk until diarrhea stops. It is important that infants continue breast-feeding and drinking water as desired while receiving these salt solutions.

---

**Hindu Poet: 6**

Hindus feel strongly about their religion. They visit their temples weekly and on holy days to bow before the symbols of their gods. They keep small shrines for worship in their homes. Taxi and bus drivers often carry images and flower garlands on their dashboards, they burn incense in their vehicles.

Hindus worship. They pray, they repeat mantras, they read scriptures. They bring offerings of flowers, rice, rupees. Hindu temples cluster with images, gods and goddesses; Krishna, Rama, Parvati, Shiva, Vishnu, Lakshmi, Kali, Brahma, Sita, Indra. There are gods for everyone, for every occasion, plenty of gods to go around, no one needs to feel left out.

Huge crowds of worshippers often gather for religious festivals, millions of worshippers. They meet to commemorate events in the lives of their favourite divinities. They make regular pilgrimages to holy rivers, the Ganges, or to other holy sites.

Some Hindus leave their regular everyday lives. They become ascetics and wander off into the forest, or the mountains, where they sit cross-legged, and sleep on the ground, and fast, and seek salvation.

Hindus are no more idolaters than Christians. They speak of the symbolic nature of their many descriptions of god.

Yet Hindus nurture a tolerance that can't be found among Christians. Hindus are happy to practise Hinduism, or Islam, or Christianity, Buddhism. Why not? The goal of all religions is the same. Different creeds, they say, only depict different paths to the same god. God may possess disparate forms, and names, and apparent contradictions, and still be one god. Hindus feel strongly about their religion.

Oooooooooooooooooommmmmmmmmmmmmmmm.

# February 15

On the road from Fatehpur we stop to photograph a dancing bear. Bear with a rope through his nose, collar round his snout. The boy, his handler, wiggles a stick, the bear dances. The boy speaks, jerks on the rope, the bear plays banjo. I turn to get back in the car, the boy demands money. We argue. One hundred rupees, he says. Ten rupees, I say. One hundred rupees, he says. The bear dances.

We drive. Stop again. Photograph a herd of cattle on the road, maybe 35, 40, steers most of them. Old, thin, every rib showing. Behind them two herders, pushing them to market. To slaughter, Mr Singh says. Mr Singh smiles. We gather that this is about Hindus, there can't be many Hindus in the region.

We stop again. Three women on the road, single file, large clay pots on their heads—orange, pink, blue, yellow, red Punjabi suits and saris. The leader turns and covers her face when she sees our camera. We feel suddenly impolite, taking pictures, wonder if we've broken some taboo. We drive again.

And then we're in Bharatpur. We take a room at the *Eagle's Nest*, lime-green hotel, they offer a room for Mr Singh too. It's clean enough, I guess, concrete, screens in the windows, most of them. Each new room in India brings an hour or two adjustment. What will we do about the dust? The bugs? Rock doves in the bathroom? We realize what we really wanted was something from Canada, new carpet, smooth sheets. Holiday Inn. Journey's End. But the *Eagle's Nest* will do.

Bharatpur. Keoladeo National Park. Bird sanctuary. We make our first trip into the park, walking. Forest. Swamp. We hire a guide for the morning. We meet Colin, we have a whisky with Colin, his own supply. Colin, a 60-year-old Scot, lives in Paris, visits in India. Colin says he loves to travel alone; still, he spends the evening with us, talks and talks. We have dinner together Eagle's Nest Restaurant. The food, quite greasy, but delicious. Susan and I worry about hygiene, flies everywhere, we saw the cooks preparing food on the floor of the kitchen as walked in, an open fire.

# KEOLADEO GHANA
# NATIONAL PARK

A birdwatcher's paradise, the Keoladeo Ghana
National Park at Bharatpur may be the finest
water-bird reserve of the world. Once a part of
the Yamuna's riverbed, this low-lying area of
some 28.7 square kilometres was developed
into a duck hunting preserve under the regime
of Maharajah Kisan Singh in 1899. It was
declared a sanctuary in 1956, upgraded to a
National Park in 1982, and became a World-
Heritage Site in 1985.

Summer in Keoladeo is tortuous and dry. The
sun bakes, the soil hardens and cracks. Lilies,
hydrilla, ipomoea wither and die. When
monsoon finally breaks in July the marsh
springs into life. Moths, mosquitoes, ants,
fireflies, grasshoppers, crickets attract frogs,
fish; attract cormorants, egrets, ibis,
kingfishers; attract harriers, vultures and kites.
Woodpeckers rattle in the kadam trees. Mynas,
hoopoes, barbets settle into their nests. Otters
splash and hunt, turtles slide from jutting logs,
snakes whisper in the grass, herds of cheetal
(spotted deer) and neelgai (blue bull) wander in
the meadows.

Keoladeo offers 353 species of birds, 120 of
these breed in the park. It is the winter home for
migrants arriving in early September and

October from central Asia and Siberia. The endangered Siberian Crane is the most eagerly awaited of these, Bharatpur remains one of its last wintering grounds.

## February 16
## Birds of India

Dab-chick or little grebe.

Large cormorant. Indian shag. Little cormorant. Darter.

Grey heron.
Purple heron. Pond heron.
Night-heron, cattle egret, large egret (our great egret?).
Median egret, little egret, white ibis, glossy ibis, painted stork,
open-bill stork, black-necked stork and spoonbill.

Greylag goose, bar-headed goose, lesser whistling teal, white-eyed
pochard, tufted pochard, ruddy shelduck, spot-billed duck, pintail,
common teal, mallard, gadwall, wigeon, shoveller (these last six just
like home), cotton teal, comb duck.

Black-winged kite, pariah kite, crested serpent-eagle, marsh harrier,
lesser spotted eagle, greater spotted eagle, ring-tailed fishing eagle,
king vulture, Indian white-backed vulture, Egyptian vulture, tawny
eagle, grey partridge, common peafowl, common crane, sarus crane,
Siberian crane, white-breasted waterhen, purple moorhen, Indian
moorhen, Chinese coot, bronze-winged jacana, painted snipe,
common snipe, white-tailed lapwing, red-wattled lapwing, black-
tailed godwit, common redshank, greenshank, common sandpiper,
wood sandpiper, golden plover, black-winged stilt, whiskered tern,
Indian lesser crested-tern, yellow-legged green pigeon, blue rock
pigeon, Indian ring-dove, little brown dove, rose-ringed parakeet,
blossom-headed parakeet, crow-pheasant, sirkeer cuckoo, collared
scops-owl, spotted owlet, brown hawk owl, barred owlet.

House swift, common kingfisher, lesser pied kingfisher, white-breasted
kingfisher, Indian three-toed kingfisher, green bee-eater, Indian
roller, hoopoe, common grey hornbill, crimson-breasted barbet, great
Himalayan barbet, Himalayan pied woodpecker, yellow-fronted pied
woodpecker, little scaly-bellied green woodpecker, wire-tailed
swallow, red-rumped swallow, dusky crag-martin, plain sand-martin,

collared sand-martin, grey shrike, bay-backed shrike, rufous-backed shrike, black drongo, white-bellied drongo, greater racket-tailed drongo, starling, common myna, pied myna, brahminy myna, house crow, jungle crow, Eurasian jay, Indian treepie.

Small minivet, fairy bluebird, white-cheeked bulbul, red-vented bulbul, jungle babbler, rufous-bellied babbler, Tickell's blue flycatcher, grey-headed flycatcher, streaked laughing-thrush, blue whistling-thrush, black-throated thrush, bar-throated siva, black-capped sibia, dull green leaf-warbler, tailorbird, bluethroat, brown rock-chat, Indian magpie-robin, orange-flanked bush-robin, pied bushchat, black redstart, Goldenstadt's redstart, grey-winged blackbird.

Grey tit, fire-capped tit, green-backed tit, yellow-cheeked tit, red-headed tit, chestnut-bellied nuthatch, wall creeper (in Rishikesh), spotted grey creeper, white wagtail, yellow-headed wagtail, large pied wagtail, masked wagtail.

Purple sunbird, Indian white-eye, house sparrow, tree sparrow, yellow-throated sparrow, white-backed munia, pink-browed rosefinch, golden-fronted finch, crested bunting. (One hundred and fifty-nine species in total,

and all the others we don't recognize.)

## February 16

India seems almost as crowded
with birds as with people. The landscape
yesterday and today still alive with waterholes
and slough, not yet perfectly flat
and drained like the farmland south
and west of Winnipeg. Progress. Farm

technology. Indian birds everywhere
here in Bharatpur. Acres of forest
and marsh. More birds than Susan
and I ever imagined. In every puddle.
Under every bush. One hundred
species in just a few hours. India

is crowded. With birds. With people.
Must be almost as many birds as people.

## Bharatpur: Susan

Seven a.m.

Our Keoladeo guide has to rush his breakfast this morning. He seems annoyed, suggests we order a meal from a roadside vendor. We haven't eaten, but we say, no. We're anxious to see birds, afraid to buy food along the roadside.

My first time on a cycle rickshaw. He pedals us through the refuge on a cycle rickshaw, what a strange and luxurious way to travel. A few times he does stop the bike and ask us to walk. Now you walk, he says. We must be very heavy.

He's so quick with the names of birds. Sometimes he borrows John's binoculars, does he really need them? I think he just wants to hold them, weigh them in his hands. Does he really know all those birds? We begin to have doubts later in the day about his identifications, make some of our own decisions.

We get hungry. We snack on pineapple-cream cookies. They've been factory packaged, we think they're safe to eat.

## MOTHER TERESA

When I was eighteen I decided to leave my
home in Skopje, Yugoslavia and become a nun;
it was my wish to work in India. I have never
doubted that I did the right thing ...

The sick and the destitute, the beggar picked
up from the streets, the leper rejected by his
family, the dying woman refused admittance to
a hospital. All will be taken in, fed, washed and
given a place to rest. Those who can be treated
will be given whatever medical attention they
require; those who are beyond treatment will be
given the opportunity to die with dignity, having
received the rituals of their faith; for Hindus,
water from the Ganges; for Muslims, readings
from the Koran; for Christians, the last rites.

In order to understand and help those who have
nothing, we must live like them ... Hail Mary full
of grace, the Lord is with thee. Blessed art thou
among women, and blessed is the fruit of thy
womb, Jesus. Holy Mary, Mother of God, pray
for us sinners now and at the hour of our death.

The poverty of the West seems far more
difficult to solve than the poverty of India ...

**February 16**

In the early afternoon we drive on. Water buffalo, the common carriers of freight in northern India, have stretched overnight to become camels; have taken a loftier view of the freight carrier's predicament, the problems of sore feet, big loads, flat tires. Women's dresses, even brighter now in the desert sun, more inclined toward gold and pink and burgundy. Men in Mussoorie wore western suits and sweaters; on the road to Jaipur men's dress becomes more traditional, white cloth and turban.

We pass through flatland, desert. Catch sudden ridges that jag from the plains to drift far into the distance, old and crumbled forts from the age of the shahs and the rajas perch high on their peaks. We pass over long bridges that reach across the flood plain, sand and dry flood plain, no water. Remember the monsoon? Thirty inches of rain will fall on this road in July and August. Water rushing under this bridge—swing and gurgle—will take unsuspecting trees, animals, humans.

Traffic swirls. Vehicles pass. Around. Beside. Between. We find a definite madness to the driving here. Never hang your elbow out the window of a car in India! Death wish. Drivers put their tractors across the highway in time for us to brake and slide. Cowherds drive their charges off the pasture onto the road just as we arrive. Buses squeeze by, force us deep into the gravel shoulder. Lorries crumble in the ditches.

**February 16**

What I haven't told you, what I'm unable able to tell you about
India.

How we count the days; just think, our home, in 16 days we'll be
home again.
How we hold our noses, shy at human feces on the road; urine smells
the same in any language.
How we hate vultures.
How we check our waiter's clothes and hands, watch how he opens and
wipes our Coke bottles, wish he wouldn't touch them at all.
How everything feels dirty.
How we gape at misshapen people, their scars, their missing limbs.
How we gawk.
How we turn away.
How we chase flies from our food.
How we twist in bed at night as killer lorries crash through our
dreams.
How we hate beggars.
How white, how western we really were.

These things may all be true. Or they may not. You can try your own
imagination.

The life Susan and I observe in India is hard to describe, even to
conceive. We think of it as poverty. Dirty. What do we really
know? What is poverty? Who is rich? Who is poor? Who
makes such decisions?

## Hindu Poet: 7

When I first saw the temples 20 years ago; marble, cave and stone
temples; red, gray, white; or painted.

When I saw the temples; charms and fecund figures carved and cut
in old and rotting stone; long drawn-out columns of
elephants and horses; swarms of birds and mammals; finest
flowers. Cobra cowls and serpent tails; leaping gods and
dancing goddesses; their bulbous breasts, distended teats,
their swollen swinging sex, cock and cunt and craving.

When I saw the temples; lovers flirting, caressing, coupling in all the
tender postures of the Kamasutra; sweethearts carved in bold
and living stone. When I saw the temples; and everywhere
around pilgrims, worshippers and devotees; pleas and
prayers and postulants.

When I first saw the temples 20 years ago, poor Mennonite boy; I
shuffled and I shook, I champed and chafed, I sweated and I
swayed; I heard the voice of god or goddess calling; heard
the voice of god and goddess, voice of temple pigeons
calling.

Oooooooooommmmmmmmmmmmm.

**February 16**

India—nine hundred million people. Canada holds only twenty-six million in three times the space. Imagine! Every time you see one person in Canada multiply times one hundred, one hundred people standing in your bedroom beside you.

Think about any similarity in the meaning of the words *tourist* and *cliche*. Everywhere we go in Agra, Bharatpur, Jaipur we see the same ten westerners, at the same ten attractions. Camera, binoculars; travelling cliches, all of us. We think of them as western, their skin looks more or less the same as ours, though they sound European; we notice things like this, hair and skin colour, in India.

We check into the Rajasthan Palace Hotel in Jaipur. Clean, comfortable, a big bed, a shower, the walls and floors are marble. Susan writes on a postcard to her parents that all Indian drivers play chicken on the highways, and that we're staying in a marble room. Susan writes five postcards, we mail them from the front desk, wonder if they'll ever get to Canada. We hand the postcards to a man at the hotel's front desk, Susan tells me that the man's staring bothers her. They don't stop, she says, even when I look back. We've heard stories, women have so little power in India.

In the early evening we go out with Mr Singh to shop for hand-woven rugs in Jaipur. The best rug shop in India, Mr Singh says, you don't need to buy. He introduces us to M-L. M-L shows us dozens of rugs. All sizes, colours, beautiful. He talks about rugs, how they're made, shows us the men and women working in the plant. We watch as rugs are knotted, washed, glazed, trimmed. Six hundred knots per square inch, M-L says. Look, he says, the weaver has committed the pattern to memory, each pattern has its own song. We argue, and haggle, and deal; buy two small hand-woven rugs. Mr Singh looks puzzled. M-L looks puzzled. They expected us to spend more money, we never spend enough money.

*Here's a list of things you can bring:*
*one can of maple syrup*
*two large bags of sunflower seeds*
*one baseball (for Jon)*
*a 1995 calendar*
*some neat posters*
*two 24 packs of AA Duracell batteries*
*one carton of Skor bars*
*two packs of red licorice*
*two pairs wool work socks*
*one Timex sports watch (for Jon)*
*some good music tapes (for Anna)*
*one pair of running shoes (Jon)*
*jeans (Anna)*
Seventeen *or* YM *magazine (Anna)*
*books (you know what we like)*

*Bring lots of warm clothes and maybe sleeping bags for yourselves. It's cold in the mountains, no central heating.*

Love

## February 17

Wake this morning to the call of a common peafowl, shriek of a peafowl outside, I take a short walk to look for him. Peacocks shouldn't be that hard to spot. I climb a set of stairs, find instead a red-wattled lapwing, happens to be nesting on the flat roof of our room. The peacock still calls somewhere in the next yard. Susan calls too, she's done her shower, she doesn't want to lose me. One of the hotel workers rests from his laundry while we stroll past. We breakfast in the dining hall of the Rajasthan Palace Hotel, we order eggs and toast, the breakfast of choice in India. The eggs arrive hard and well-done, no salmonella. We've been warned that salmonella is especially risky with eggs in India. I wonder though if in three days I could teach our waiter and cook something about *over easy*.

We visit the City Fort and the museum. We wonder at the windows and screens of the Hawa Mahal, where courtesans once admired returning soldiers. Lakshmi, the elephant, wrenches and rolls us up the hill to the Amber Palace. All these ruins, forts, palaces; intricate, elaborate, labyrinthine. Landscaped for gardens and pools and comfort, thick-walled, high-ceilinged, cool in the heat of the afternoon. The restaurants we visit in the evening offer air-conditioning, abundant and exotic fare.

We've really made it, haven't we, Susan and I. We have a private car, Ambassador. We have our own driver. We say: Drive, Mr Singh; he drives. We say: Stop, Mr Singh; he stops. If we're worried, Mr Singh always knows what to do. We carry a bottle of Bisleri water and a camera case. We shop, we bargain. We have bought a few things, souvenirs, objects to lay on our mantel at home. We ride Lakshmi up and down the hill near Amber Palace. We are wealthy foreigners, this is how *we* live in India.

I cannot forget this: Twenty years ago I saw India from crowded fourth-class trains and buses, now I see the same place tourist upper class. Riding down the hill again from the fort, I joke with the elephant driver. I ask if his elephant ever disobeys. Does Lakshmi ever disobey? Never, he says. And then he slashes across her neck with a heavy box-hook, I see the scars from the hook on the elephant's neck.

**February 17**

Sometimes we wonder what Mr Singh thinks of us. Does he question why we didn't buy a bigger carpet? Can he accept that we too have limited resources? Can he understand our relationship to the children, that they have two sets of parents? Does he find us arrogant, or unfriendly? Is he getting tired of us?

## February 18

The main streets of Jaipur swarm with vehicles and people; bicycles, cars, camels, motorcycles, horses, trucks, pedestrians. Traffic pours from the side streets. Traffic reels, eddies in the roundabouts. Traffic roars through city gates. Susan and I turn to the camera, our fingers ache for the buttons on our camera, our desire to document, to remember. We long to photograph these faces, the clothes and colours, the jumble of the Jaipur streets. And the weddings— February is the month for weddings. But people turn from our camera, we can't take a picture in Jaipur without catching somebody close-up, that seems more and more impolite. We've been told that many Indians object to being photographed, others think they should be paid, we feel torn between these warnings and our curiosity.

We stop at Jantra Mantra, an astronomical astrological observatory and garden; built by Emperor Jai Singh, 1730. Stars and moons and planets, birth and death, fortune, fate. I'm excited by the complexity of the instruments, huge steel and concrete instruments; we're allowed to photograph for 50 rupees. Ahead of us Susan and I notice another kind of picture; two young men holding hands. Everywhere in India teenage boys hold hands with teenage boys, girls hold hands with girls, men with men. They feel no fear, no shame. What do we teach our young in Canada?

Later, at Jaigarh Fort, a bevy of government cars and officials winds through the narrow lanes and up the hill to see the *Big Gun*, the largest cannon in the world. This cannon they say was only fired once; when the Jaigarh enemies realized its power they deserted the battleground and fled. But even here, at Jaigarh Fort, standing under the barrel of the big gun, two soldiers hold hands while on duty.

The landscape north of Jaipur reminds us of New Mexico, when we drove through two years ago. Hills, ridges, cactus, desert vegetation, and the same red earth. We remember the pueblo and the cave dwellings. All the buildings, forts, palaces in Jaipur dressed in the same red tone as New Mexico a half-world away.

## February 18

Jaipur;
a young city,
a planned city, a city
of astrological signs
and symbols, rectangular
city, city of forts,
palaces, a city
of bazaars, city
for shoppers, city of jewels
and carpets,
a city of elephants, of camels,
city of weddings, pink
city, city of crowds
and noise,
and beggars, city of
kings and courtesans, city
of lavish daydreams
for Western visitors.

## Men Staring: Susan

I expected the men to stare, but I hadn't expected *how* they stare.

I feel invaded, even when I meet their eyes they won't look away. I won't go anywhere alone. I feel my anger building, they seem to enjoy my discomfort. I learn to sit with my back to the rest of the room.

They only stop if John stares back at them. I hope they're afraid of him.

# LOCAL TRANSPORT

Jaipur offers a well established and varied system of public transport. Tourist taxis can be hired throughout the city, either at taxi stands or with the help of tourist agencies or hotels. These are especially useful for sightseeing on a half or full-day basis. Rates generally vary with demand.

Auto rickshaws are available at railway stations, at bus stands and in the city centre. Cycle rickshaws, the most commonly used carrier, provide excellent short distance transport. You may, if you're fortunate, find a horse tonga waiting at the street corner. Rates for rickshaws and tongas are always negotiable.

The city bus service affords the cheapest mode of transport within the city and suburbs. Of course, buses do get a bit crowded at times.

Check with the staff at your hotel. They may be able to help you in renting your own personal bicycle.

**February 18**

*India? Why India?* That's how I started my journal 20 years ago, it was the question everyone asked. India, what *was* I looking for? An answer? An intuition? A gesture of hope? Enlightenment is such a long word. I wanted to be happy. The tourist guides and books all promised that. Peace. Discovery. Was that what I found?

This passage to India offers a much more sensible route. I've come to visit my kids. I'll stop at a bird sanctuary, put a few notes in my diary. I'm older than I was 20 years ago. Do you see that? I feel happy now. Happy enough. Twenty years ago every question carried such a huge weight.

*I will never be the same.* That's what I wrote then, I suppose my twenties felt like that. But I haven't changed that much, have I? My face more wrinkled; my hair shorter, scarce, a bit more gray. I'm a few pounds heavier. Small changes, nothing clear or obvious, it's hard to draw the line that brings contentment.

**February 19, 1995**

At five in the morning, the Jaipur/Delhi highway drives like a nightmare. Hundreds of lorries, buses, cars. Dark, and dust, and headlights. Two lanes, sometimes three, bumper mocking bumper. Many accidents.

In Delhi our accommodation has failed. We can't find rooms, not at $25, not at $250. Still, we choose to be fussy; terrible, terrible Westerners. We have come to Delhi expecting better accommodation, instead it's not as good as Jaipur, and far more expensive. The rooms we do finally see are dirty, the carpets smell, the hot water barely warm, dust lies thick in the cabinets.

Desperate, we call a contact, a professor at the Delhi University; it's Sunday, we call his home. A young man answers the phone and invites us to the house, he says his father will be back soon. The professor, a short man, very dark-skinned, a generous host, tells us that he's from the south. He teases us. He makes jokes about his ethnic origins. He says his wife, a professor in Sanskrit, comes from the north. He says between them they know dozens of languages, but only one in common, English. We drink tea. Finally, he makes arrangements for us at the YMCA.

Later, in our room, we have time to feel shame for our lack of courage, our ingratitude.

## Hindu Poet: 8

That sadhu,
with his prayer
beads and his sacred
thread, his painted
forehead, with his
matted hair, his
naked limbs, penis
dangling in the open air; that
sadhu, in the
courtyard
of the temple, there,
in Varanasi, he's got
one foot
in the holy
Ganga, one foot
on the sacred bank, holds
his arms up high and
shakes them, gives out
a bellow; that sadhu,
is he mad? d'you think
he's mad? why is
he shouting? d'you
think he's
shouting at the
gods?

Ooooommmmmm.

**February 20**

A different world in Delhi. We meet professors, writers, teachers,
librarians. I prepare to read for the Indian Association of
Canadian Studies and worry suddenly about relocation of the
English language. A gesture on the road to Flag Hill east of
Mussoorie, a canvas-backed jeep, will anyone understand
me? What signs and arrows will I need to post for my
Eastern travellers.

The reading. Susan and I are treated with great honour. Our Indian
hosts compliment us, handle us like royalty. The Indian
audience loves to challenge, Indians love to talk, love the
sound of words. They ask me to read certain poems again.
They talk about the lines I've just read, they tickle them
inside out, tell me what those lines are about, they seem to
notice every word. Wonderful to get all this attention.

I read again in the evening at the India International Centre. Another
friendly audience, they invite Susan to speak too. Suddenly
one of the listeners asks me to sing. Something from Bob
Dylan, he says. *How many seas must a white dove sail ...*
Later our hosts offer us hors d'oeuvres and dainties, just like
in Canada.

And I worried about language, I've never felt so understood.

## February 21

The YMCA Blue Triangle in Delhi begins to feel like home. We've hung our clothes in the closets. We've placed our books beside the travel alarm on the night table, our shoes in the alley. We've sent out the laundry. The faces at the front desk smile as we walk by, we feel they look familiar. We've spoken to one of the blue-jacketed men on our floor and paid him R100 to take the carpet from our room and clean the floor.

Today, Susan and I were to travel to Meerut to take part in a conference on writing. That conference has been postponed because of rioting and violence, still the same battle as when we passed through with Mr Singh. Instead of Meerut, we take the Delhi Tour. We visit the Lakshmi Narayan Temple, the towers of Qutab Minar, then the Muslim temple—Jama Masjid, the Red Fort, Parliament, the India Gate, Raj Ghat, the National Gallery of Modern Art; such a mix of religious, political, cultural icons, ancient and modern. We lunch at the five star Meridian Hotel. Very posh. The food is good, and expensive. One of the Germans on the tour gets angry about the price of Meridian food, he pouts all afternoon, his girlfriend goes to sit with someone else.

Fun tonight at the home of Canadian High Commission staff, Nesrin and Jeremias. I drink Indian rum. Chandra—our reading host and agent and friend, Secretary of the Indian Association for Canadian Studies—Chandra drinks wine. We joke and tease. Chandra giggles.

I'm really looking forward to you guys coming, we'll have a great time. By the time you get here Mussoorie should be quite peaceful again.

Yes, I have found bird books at the local bookstore. You better get in shape though; if you want to see birds we'll have to go for a bit of a hike, I see only crows here at the school. We've booked a guest room at Edgehill for you. Do you want Anna or I to stay with you overnight while you're here? Anna and I will plan for things to do when you come. If you like, we can go for an overnight hike. And I'm sure you'll want to visit the bazaar.

When you arrive at the Delhi airport you'll pick up your luggage and go through Customs. Turn right after Customs, you'll see a bank where you can change some money. Change about $200 Cdn. To your left you'll see a counter where you can get a taxi. Pay for the taxi at the counter, about R100, they will bargain with you. Take the taxi to the YWCA International Guesthouse at 10 Parliament Street. We have reserved a room for you. Mr Man Mohan Singh will pick you up at 6 a.m. He will carry a note for you from us, he will bring you here to the school in relative safety and comfort.

Love

**February 22**

Time falls quickly now, like dominoes, like house crows from a shadow sky.

We meet with a young poet in the morning, he brings a gift to honour us, tradition. He says he's Jain, he lives at home. He talks about his restlessness and his age, he's just turned 28, he thinks he should be settled by now, he wants advice. His struggle sounds familiar to me, I remember my anxious years. I tell him I'm sure his disquiet will pass. But that may be a poor guess, what do I really know about young Jain men in India.

Tonight, dinner at Chandra's house. His wife is shy, she prepares food and serves us, she eats in the kitchen. We're surprised to learn that they too boil their drinking water. Surprised how hard their children—son and daughter—study; four hours before, four hours after school, highschool. Like their parents, they must get the best education. PhD.

Chandra's company becoming more and more delightful. Chandra loves to laugh and tease, loves to chuckle. A happy friendly man. Susan snaps a picture of Chandra and I giggling together.

# NEW DELHI

India's capital, gateway to a vibrant country, contemporary Delhi has grown into a business metropolis effectively combining both the ancient and the modern.

Over 3,000 years seven successive dynasties have chosen this one location for their seat of power. Delhi constitutes a blend of seven older cities; among them Lalkot, Siri, Lodis, Ferozabad, Shahjahanabad. The difference between Old and New Delhi today reflects the difference between the capitals of the Mughals and the British.

Wherever visitors choose to explore in modern Delhi they will confront the variables of past and present, a diversity of cultures and people, a spirited city striving for the best of the twenty-first century.

## February 23

Ferozabad, Shahjahanabad, such ordinary syllables, exotic images, the song of those names on my tongue.

Our visit to the Mughal Gardens this morning very disappointing. Heavy security, is it the prime minister's house nearby? Soldiers strip us of our camera and binoculars, herd us along a concrete path, past arrow markers. If we step two feet to one side, they wave their guns at us. I get angry and shout at them because of the binoculars; we had hoped to find some birds, just a few more species before we leave for Canada.

In the afternoon we shop with the beautiful Sudha. Sudha wears a green Punjabi suit, pink shawl, a gold band on her ring finger, takes us to a real Delhi bazaar. Outdoor. Bargains, bargains, bargains. A sweater for me, a gray Punjabi suit for Susan.

Everything turns on itself. Home. To airport. To home. Fly to India. To Canada. To India. Back to Canada. So little time between. One punjabi suit breeds another. Last night I dreamt of my books and violins. In two days we'll be home again.

## Appliances: Susan

No computer.
No TV. Or
fax. Only
dial phones,
and they
never ring
for us. That's
good!

# Hindu Poet: 9

The holy river Ganga, the goddess Ganga, she flows from the
      Himalayas, flows from the snows and the evergreen trees,
      born from the cold and the mountains;
The roaring river Ganga, falls through deep gorges, rattles through
      chasms and canyons;
The goddess Ganga, whom Hindus worship, whom Hindus flock to
      honour and worship; where Hindus bathe and Hindus gather,
      where Hindus drink;
The mother Ganga, the millions of pilgrims to Ganga, pilgrims who
      die on the shores of the Ganga, whose ashes scatter in the
      Ganga, half-burned bodies floating in the Ganga, sadhus
      bodies tied to rocks and drowned in the Ganga;
Holy river Ganga, river of the Indian people, river of Indian history,
      river of rajas and moguls, river of poor and of peasant,
      defeat and victory, Mother Ganga, river of moods and
      seasons, river that winds lazy through plains, river of desert,
      dries to a desert;
The Goddess Ganga, river of monsoon, river that rises and rises,
      river that floods, raging river, river that ravages village and
      hut, carries down cattle, and crops, Mother Goddess Ganga;
Holy Mother Ganga, giver of nourishment and death, giver of fertile
      silt and erosion, river that runs deep into the sea, river that
      washes chemical waste into the sea, river that washes the
      waste from distilleries, refineries, mills and factories,
      cyanide, arsenic, lead, zinc, selenium, chromium, mercury,
      cadmium, phosphorus, nitrogen sulphate, carries them far
      into the sea;
The holy river Ganga, har har Ganga, hai Ganga, dearest Ganga,
      Ooooooooooooommmmmmmmmmmmmmmmmmmmmmmmm.

## February 23

All our
fears about
illness; we

drink
only tea,
or mineral water;
never
eat raw
vegetables, eat no
meat, never
miss
our malaria
pills, (hundred

dollars worth
of pills, saw
no more than
two
or three
mosquitoes); we have

not been
sick
once.

## February 23

Chandra says that some people see only ugliness in
       India. There is lots of that, he says, ugliness. He hopes
       that we have found some beauty as well.

Goodbye Chandra, we hate to say goodbye to Chandra.

## February 24, 1995

Three a.m.

Airport! This is the one word all taxi drivers know. In India they seem to know few others. Is it our speech? The places we go? Our drivers in Delhi never seem to understand us, always get lost, need to ask directions.

Airport? Yes, yes? That one word and we are gone.

Sunrise. Through the window I see a river winding. A flood plain. Mountains. Varieties of rock formations, red and brown. Slabs, peaks, ridges. Passes and plateaus. Pakistan. Afghanistan. I see desert. Imagine the chatter of the cactus wren. Later through the snow I see trees spotting a slope. Above Samarkand our plane arches slowly to the west. Sun still sparkling on the ice caps; this sun won't set now until just before we reach home. Air Canada.

We study the CBC news; three weeks without, nothing much changes. Budgets. Layoffs. The cost of the rail strike. The NHL and players have settled. We survey hockey scores. Then Heathrow. Suddenly we feel at home again. I think of Paul Bickle, violinmaker, my one friend in England. Paul, dead before he turned 40.

Hours later, the lights of Winnipeg, and the Beatles singing over the intercom. *I hope you know by now* ... The longest day of our lives, and the shortest. Thirty-two hours. Twelve time zones. Half a world again. Half a universe. India to home.

Eleven p.m.

## March 13, 1995

The sun sets in the evening, wakes again
each morning. The moon follows. Wind
swirls and howls over hills, through
trees, round corners. Rain
scorns all fences, all boundaries.
Red-tailed hawk pairs, after migration,

return to the same nest year
after year. They renovate; add
a few twigs, branches, dried
grass. That Baltimore
oriole stops at the same
neighbour's backyard every

spring. If his nectar jar
isn't swinging from the clothesline,
he teeters, whistles, scolds, dips
his head till the homeowner
notices. I have found no
good reason for my preoccupations

with India; what brought me there, when
I will return, I'm sure now
that I'll return. The sun falls
in the evening. Wakes
again. The moon chases. Wind
swirls over hills, through

trees. Rain ignores most boundaries, scorns
even these established boundaries.

## First Appendix

Our Indian acquaintances get so excited when they learn that I visited India 20 years ago. They want to know how things have changed. You must observe many changes, they say. How would you say India has changed?

To be honest, I don't notice many changes. India doesn't look that different after all these years. I see a few newer cars; the Suzuki Marati looks new, looks like a car you might see in 1995 in North America. The other cars, the buses, trucks, motorcycle taxis, they look just like in 1975. The landscape looks the same. The people look the same, their dress. The Taj Mahal looks more or less the same. But that's not the answer our hosts want to hear.

It's hard to compare one time and place to another. Maybe if we'd landed in Calcutta just like I did the first time, if we'd retraced every step. Maybe if we'd travelled ordinary class. Maybe if the temperatures had stretched into the 40s. Or if we'd stayed longer. Maybe *I've* changed too much. I try to give the right answers, I want to be a good guest, I want the Indian people to like me. Eventually, my examiners offer the words they'd like to hear. Industry, population, pollution, they say. So many changes.

Here at home, here in my own room months later, I begin to see India more clearly. I begin to see change, take the time to compare an old memory to a young one.

## Second Appendix

Buying rugs. Those beautiful rugs. For R16,000 we could have bought a huge oriental rug, they offered to ship it home for us. I feel like a fool now, R16,000 is less than $800. It's not till we get home that I realize how wary and suspicious I was, how those rupee notes clung to my fingers.

## Third Appendix

A boy approaches me in Connaught Place. He's dark, skin and eyes, young—maybe seven, maybe eight. Hair unkempt. Castoffs for clothes. Gray pants, gray striped shirt. He carries a bag, white plastic bag, that hangs heavy in one corner. Would you like a shoeshine, Sahib? he says. He looks straight up at me, he speaks good English.

I ignore him. It's often that way in India; beggars, hawkers surprise you, you don't know what to say. I look at my shoes, they're filthy.

A shoeshine, Sahib, he says. I will make your shoes look new, he says.

How much? I say. Maybe that will be the solution. How much do you charge? I say, five rupees?

You don't have to pay me anything, he says. I will do the job. If you think the job is good you can pay whatever you like, he says.

Where are you from? the boy says. Are you a business man? Are you American? I am a business man too, he says, I shine shoes. He pulls a rag and a big black brush from his plastic bag. But I don't do very well, he says. You see, he says and he lifts the plastic bag, I don't own a shoeshine box.

The boy spreads his black polish on my tired shoes. I can't afford a shoeshine box, he says. If I had a shoeshine box, I could set it on the street corner. People would notice me, I would do a much better business. I would be successful. What is a business man without a place to do business, he says. The boy speaks slowly, he thinks about each word.

By now the left shoe is almost done. The boy scratches at a spot of paint on the toe of the shoe. How much does a shoeshine box cost? I say. I guess I know what's coming.

## A Selection Of Our Titles In Print

**Your bookseller can order our books from General Distribution Services**, 30 Lesmills Rd, Don Mills ON M3B 2T6: Toronto ph 416 445-3333; Ont./Que. 1-800-387-0141; Atlantic/Western Canada 1-800-387-0172; USA 1-800-805-1083. Sales representation by the Literary Press Group of Canada, www.lpg.ca or info@lpg.ca. Direct from the publisher, individual orders must be prepaid. Add $2 shipping for one book ($9.95 and up) and $1 per additional item. Canadian orders must add 7% GST/HST.

**MARITIMES ARTS PROJECTS PRODUCTIONS**
BOX 506 STN A
FREDERICTON NB E3B 5A6          Ph/fax: 506 454-5127
CANADA                          E-mail: jblades@nbnet.nb.ca